MY BODY HAS
MY BODY HAS
LEGS
AND FEET

AMY CULLIFORD

A Crabtree Roots Plus Book

CRABTREE
Publishing Company
www.crabtreebooks.com

School-to-Home Support for Caregivers and Teachers

This book helps children grow by letting them practice reading. Here are a few guiding questions to help the reader with building his or her comprehension skills. Possible answers appear here in red.

Before Reading:

• What do I think this book is about?
  - *I think this book is about legs and feet.*
  - *I think this book is about how our legs and feet work.*

• What do I want to learn about this topic?
  - *I want to learn about all the ways we use our legs and feet.*
  - *I want to learn how legs and feet move.*

During Reading:

• I wonder why...
  - *I wonder why humans have two legs and two feet.*
  - *I wonder why feet have toes.*

• What have I learned so far?
  - *I have learned that knees help legs bend.*
  - *I have learned that our toes help us balance.*

After Reading:

• What details did I learn about this topic?
  - *I have learned that legs and feet are parts of our body.*
  - *I have learned that feet can be big or small.*

• Read the book again and look for the vocabulary words.
  - *I see the word **knee** on page 10 and the word **balance** on page 20. The other vocabulary words are found on page 23.*

You have two **legs**.

They are part of
your **body**.

Legs help you
move around.

Sarah uses her legs to walk to school.

I use my legs to run!

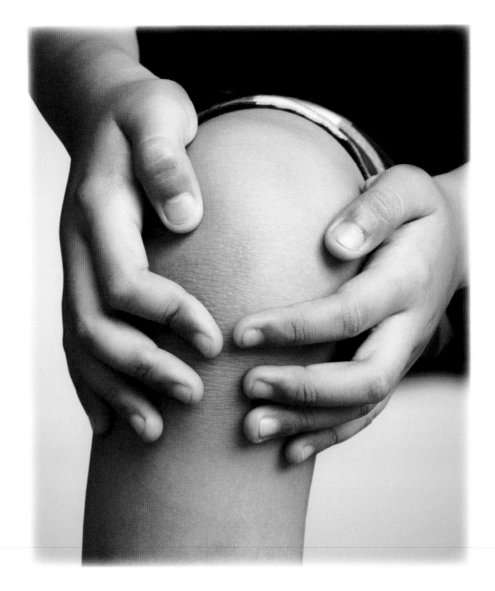

Each leg has a **knee**.

Your knees help your legs **bend**.

I use my legs and knees to jump!

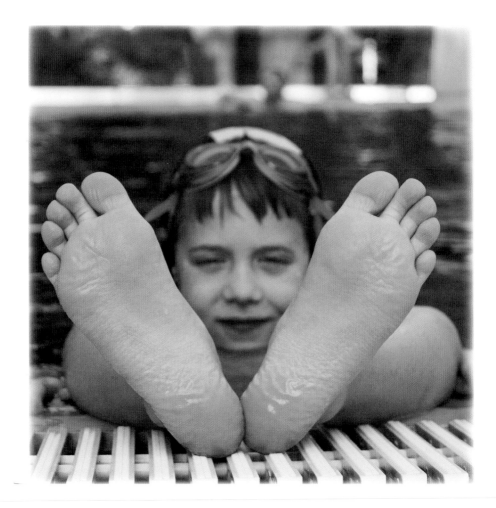

You have two feet.

Feet can be big
or small.

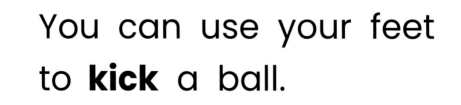

You can use your feet
to **kick** a ball.

I use my feet to play **soccer**!

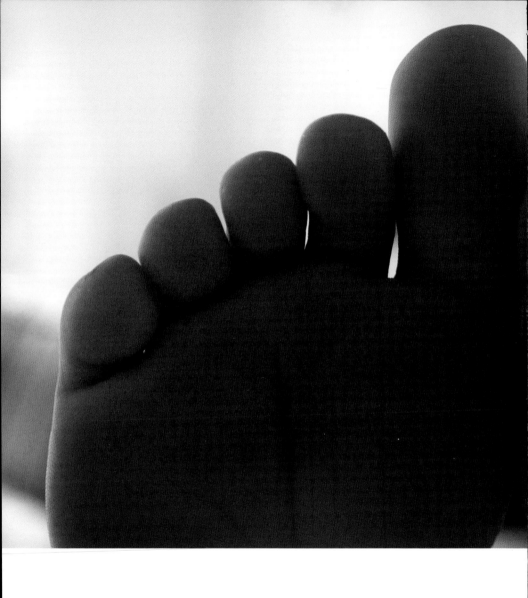

Your feet have toes.

Your toes help
you **balance**.

Word List
Sight Words

a	I	they
and	jump	to
are	knees	toes
around	leg	two
ball	legs	use
be	move	uses
big	my	walk
can	of	you
each	or	your
feet	part	
has	play	
have	run	
help	school	
her	small	

Words to Know

balance

bend

body

kick

knee

legs

soccer

MY BODY
MY BODY HAS
LEGS AND FEET

Written by: Amy Culliford

Designed by: Rhea Wallace

Series Development: James Earley

Proofreader: Janine Deschenes

Educational Consultant: Marie Lemke M.Ed.

Print and production coordinator:

Katherine Berti

Photographs:
Shutterstock: Zurijeta: cover, p. 3; Mark Nazh: p. 5;
Igor Pushkarev: p. 7; Tinnapong: p. 8; jeffy11390: p. 10;
Maarten Zeehandelaar: p. 11; Lightfield Studio: p. 13;
LeicherOliver: p. 14; Halfpoint: p. 15; Fotokostic: p. 16;
Nirat.pix: p. 17; Bricolage: p. 18; Jurrah Mesin: p. 21

Library and Archives Canada Cataloguing in Publication

Available at the Library and Archives Canada

Library of Congress Cataloging-in-Publication Data

Available at the Library of Congress

Crabtree Publishing Company

Printed in the U.S.A./CG20210915/012022

www.crabtreebooks.com   1-800-387-7650

Published in the United States
Crabtree Publishing
347 Fifth Avenue, Suite 1402-145
New York, NY, 10016

Published in Canada
Crabtree Publishing
616 Welland Ave.
St. Catharines, Ontario L2M 5V6